# SEA GIANTS OF
# DINOSAUR TIME

BY **"DINO" DON LESSEM**

ILLUSTRATIONS BY **JOHN BINDON**

 **LERNER PUBLICATIONS COMPANY / MINNEAPOLIS**

*To Brian Joseph, my first friend, who has nothing whatsoever to do with anything in this book*

Text copyright © 2005 by Dino Don, Inc.
Illustrations copyright © 2005 by John Bindon
The photographs in this book appear courtesy of: © The National History Museum, London, pp. 24, 27, 28–29.

*This book is available in two editions:*
Library binding by Lerner Publications Company,
    a division of Lerner Publishing Group
Softcover by First Avenue Editions,
    an imprint of Lerner Publishing Group
241 First Avenue North
Minneapolis, MN 55401 U.S.A

Website address: www.lernerbooks.com


Library of Congress Cataloging-in-Publication-Data

Lessem, Don.
    Sea giants of dinosaur time / by Don Lessem ; illustrations by John Bindon.
       p.   cm. — (Meet the dinosaurs)
    Includes index.
    ISBN: 0–8225–1425–7 (lib. bdg. : alk. paper)
    ISBN: 0–8225–2623–9 (pbk. : alk. paper)
    1. Marine animals, Fossil—Juvenile Literature. 1. Bindon, John, ill. II. Title. III. Series: Lessem, Don. Meet the dinosaurs.
    QE766.L47  2005
    567.9—dc22                                          2004017916

Manufactured in the United States of America
1 2 3 4 5 6 – DP – 10 09 08 07 06 05

# TABLE OF CONTENTS

# MEET THE SEA GIANTS

**WELCOME, DINOSAUR FANS!**

I'm "Dino" Don. I LOVE dinosaurs. And I love the other weird animals that lived during dinosaur time. While dinosaurs ruled the land, giant reptiles ruled the seas. Come meet these amazing ocean animals. You won't even get your feet wet!

***ARCHELON* (AHR-kuh-lahn)**
Length: 12 feet
Home: western North America
Time: 70 million years ago

***ICHTHYOSAURUS* (IHK-thee-uh-SAWR-uhs)**
Length: 6 feet
Home: western Europe, North America
Time: 180 million years ago

***KRONOSAURUS* (KROH-nuh-SAWR-uhs)**
Length: 42 feet
Home: northeastern Australia
Time: 120 million years ago

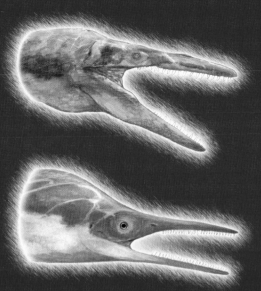

**MOSASAURUS (MOH-suh-SAWR-uhs)**
Length: 45 feet
Home: North America
Time: 65 million years ago

**OPTHALMOSAURUS (AHP-thahl-muh-SAWR-uhs)**
Length: 11 feet
Home: western Europe, North and South America
Time: 150 million years ago

**PLESIOSAURUS (PLEE-zee-uh-SAWR-uhs)**
Length: 8 feet
Home: western Europe
Time: 180 million years ago

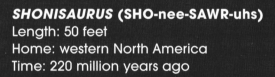

**SHONISAURUS (SHO-nee-SAWR-uhs)**
Length: 50 feet
Home: western North America
Time: 220 million years ago

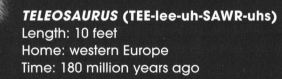

**TELEOSAURUS (TEE-lee-uh-SAWR-uhs)**
Length: 10 feet
Home: western Europe
Time: 180 million years ago

# WATER WONDERS

We are deep underwater 120 million years ago. Two huge *Kronosaurus* battle for a large fish. Each *Kronosaurus* is as long as an ice cream truck. Snap! One *Kronosaurus* grabs the fish with its sharp-toothed jaws.

Does *Kronosaurus* sound like a dinosaur name? It isn't. *Kronosaurus* was a giant sea **reptile.** Many kinds of giant sea reptiles lived in the time of dinosaurs.

# THE TIME OF THE SEA GIANTS

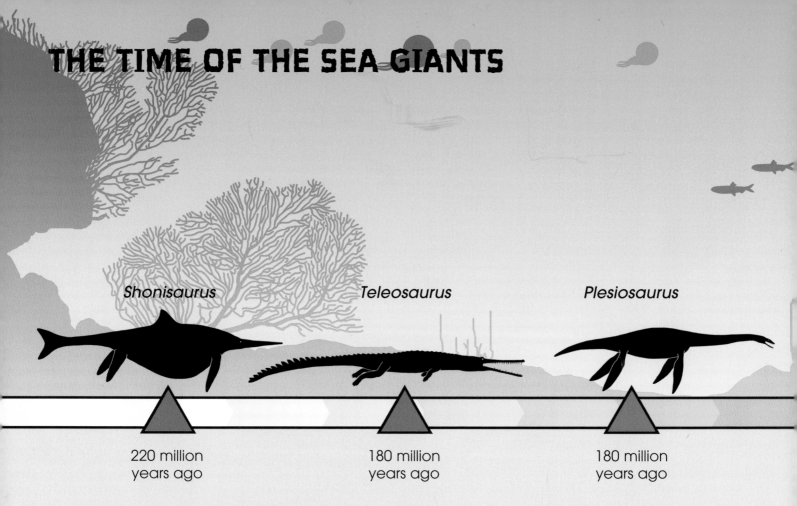

Shonisaurus

Teleosaurus

Plesiosaurus

220 million
years ago

180 million
years ago

180 million
years ago

Giant sea reptiles were not dinosaurs.
Dinosaurs came into the water only for a swim.
But sea reptiles lived in the water. Dinosaurs
had arms and legs. But most sea reptiles had
flippers. Baby dinosaurs hatched from eggs.
But at least some kinds of sea reptiles were
born live.

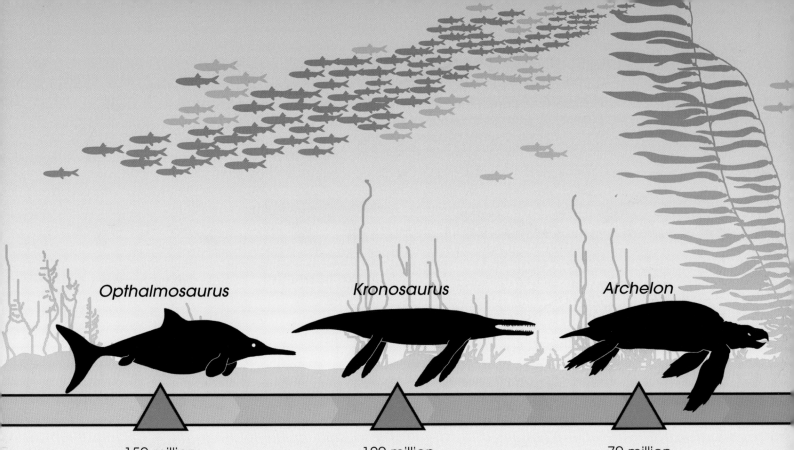

Opthalmosaurus

Kronosaurus

Archelon

150 million
years ago

120 million
years ago

70 million
years ago

Like all reptiles, the sea giants had scaly skin.
All sea reptiles breathed air with their lungs.
But sea reptiles were different from each other.
Some were **predators** that hunted fish. Others
ate eggs. Some were shaped like dolphins.
Other sea reptiles had long necks and bodies.
And still others had short, thick bodies.

# SEA GIANT FOSSIL FINDS

The numbers on the map on page 11 show some of the places where people have found fossils of the giant sea reptiles in this book. You can match each number on the map to the name and picture of the sea reptiles on this page.

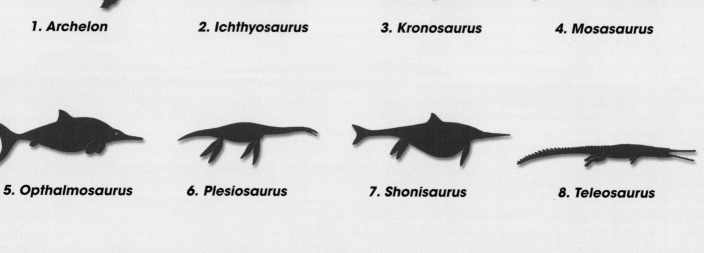

1. Archelon

2. Ichthyosaurus

3. Kronosaurus

4. Mosasaurus

5. Opthalmosaurus

6. Plesiosaurus

7. Shonisaurus

8. Teleosaurus

How do we know about the sea giants? For hundreds of years, people have found and studied the traces sea reptiles left behind when they died. **Fossils** of bones, eggs, and teeth have shown us how the giants looked and lived. So far, we've discovered hundreds of giant sea reptiles.

Giant sea reptiles lived in all of the world's oceans. So why does this map show sea reptiles on land? Some places were underwater during sea giant time. Scientists have found fossils in those places. It's too hard to look for fossils at the bottom of the ocean!

# LIFE IN THE SEA

How did the sea giants survive in the ocean?
Finding enough food wasn't easy for such
large animals. But they had many different
ways of hunting.

The sea grows dark late in the day. But
*Opthalmosaurus* chooses this time to hunt.
With its big eyes, this giant sea reptile can
see well in dark water. The fish it chases
don't see it coming—until it's too late.

*Archelon* uses huge flippers to move itself quickly through the water. It attacks a group of jellyfish. The jaws of *Archelon* are not strong. Its beak has no teeth. The soft jellyfish are a perfect food for this giant.

*Archelon* was the largest turtle of dinosaur time. It didn't have the heavy shell of the turtles we know. Instead, its shell was made of bony ribs that were covered with rubbery skin.

*Teleosaurus* swishes quickly through the
water.  Its short legs are tucked up against
its body.  It is as long as a large rowboat.
This sea crocodile closes in on a squid.
*Teleosaurus* snaps up the squid with long,
narrow jaws full of pointy teeth.

Since before the time of the dinosaurs, crocodiles have lived in rivers and swamps around the world. In dinosaur time, some crocodiles grew longer than school buses. And some swam out in the deep ocean, as *Teleosaurus* did.

*Mosasaurus* opens its powerful jaws. It is hunting a slow ammonite. The ammonite's thick shell can't protect it against *Mosasaurus*. The sea giant crushes the shellfish with its sharp, cone-shaped teeth.

*Mosasaurus* was one of the biggest and deadliest sea giants of all. This ocean hunter grew to more than 45 feet long. That's longer than a *Tyrannosaurus rex!*

*Plesiosaurus* searches for groups of fish to eat. This sea giant could reach far with its long neck to grab fish. Then *Plesiosaurus* might have dived to the seafloor to swallow rocks.

Why did it eat rocks?  The rocks tumbled around in the sea reptile's stomach.  They helped grind up the fish that *Plesiosaurus* ate. And perhaps they added weight to help *Plesiosaurus* swim longer underwater.

A group of *Shonisaurus* called a **pod** swims through the water. The pod surrounds a school of fish. Working together, the huge sea reptiles herd the fish and snap them up.

*Shonisaurus* was one of the biggest of all sea reptiles. Its body stretched longer than half a tennis court! Scientists think that *Shonisaurus* may have lived in pods, like dolphins. But it didn't swim the way dolphins do. *Shonisaurus* moved its tail from side to side. Dolphins flap their tail up and down.

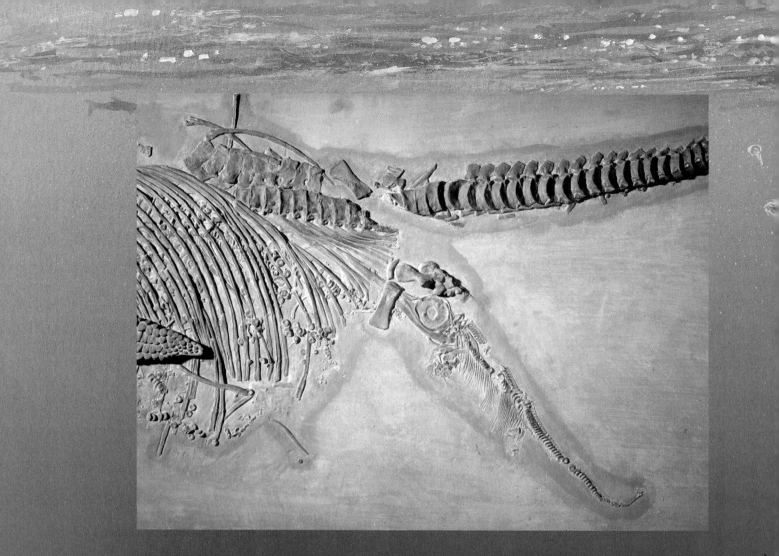

Fossils show us how some sea reptiles were born. This photo shows a small baby flowing out from under the tail of a dolphinlike sea reptile. *Ichthyosaurus* is giving birth! The baby swims freely from the moment it is born. It searches for small ocean creatures to eat.

An adult *Ichthyosaurus* was much smaller than *Shonisaurus*. The tiny babies of *Ichthyosaurus* could not protect themselves. Two or three were born at one time. That way, at least one might escape becoming dinner for a predator.

# WHAT HAPPENED TO THE SEA GIANTS?

The great sea reptiles disappeared 65 million years ago. The last of the dinosaurs died out then too. What killed them? Many scientists think that changes in Earth's weather made it hard for huge animals to find enough food.

The coast of England is one of the best places to find fossils of sea giants. Fossils have taught us many things about how the giant sea reptiles lived. We've even learned from fossil poop! It shows that *Ichthyosaurus* ate fish.

Most fossils are not found by scientists. Nearly 200 years ago in England, a boy named Joseph Anning found a strange skull in the cliffs near his home. A year later, his 12-year-old sister Mary found the rest of the skeleton. It was the first known *Ichthyosaurus*!

This photo shows Mary's *Ichthyosaurus* discovery. That skeleton wasn't her only great discovery. She also found a *Plesiosaurus* and many other fossils. Mary's amazing finds created great interest in **paleontology,** the science of studying ancient life.

Are sea reptiles like *Plesiosaurus* still swimming deep in our oceans or lakes? Many people think so. They tell stories of seeing giant reptiles in Loch Ness in Scotland and Lake Champlain in the northeastern United States. But there is no proof that these animals exist.

Large animals may live deep in Earth's waters. But they are not living plesiosaurs. Sea reptiles died out 65 million years ago. They can never come back. We can only imagine how amazing they were.

# GLOSSARY

**fossils (FAH-suhlz):** the remains, tracks, or traces of something that lived long ago

**paleontology (PAY-lee-uhn-TAH-luh-jee):** the study of ancient living things from their fossils

**pod (PAHD):** a small group of animals that swim and eat together

**predators (PREH-duh-turz):** animals that hunt and eat other animals

**reptile (REHP-tyl):** an animal that has scaly skin and breathes air with its lungs

# INDEX